Edward Henry Reynolds

The Standard Guide to St. Augustine and Fort Marion

Practical Information for Tourists, Descriptions of all Points of Interests

Edward Henry Reynolds

The Standard Guide to St. Augustine and Fort Marion
Practical Information for Tourists, Descriptions of all Points of Interests

ISBN/EAN: 9783337193560

Printed in Europe, USA, Canada, Australia, Japan

Cover: Foto ©Lupo / pixelio.de

More available books at **www.hansebooks.com**

RUINS OF GATEWAY.

SEASON OF 1885-86.

THE
STANDARD GUIDE
TO
ST. AUGUSTINE
AND
FORT MARION.

PRACTICAL INFORMATION FOR TOURISTS, DESCRIPTIONS OF ALL POINTS OF
INTEREST; AND AN HISTORICAL SUMMARY, WITH MAPS AND PLANS.

FORTY ILLUSTRATIONS FROM ORIGINAL DRAWINGS

By ROGER DAVIS.

Rede me and be nott wrothe
For J saye no thynge but trothe.—1570.

EDITED AND PUBLISHED BY

E. H. REYNOLDS,
SAINT AUGUSTINE,
FLORIDA.

TO THE READER.

IVING practical information and such descriptions as, it is hoped, may enable one to intelligently see the town, THE STANDARD GUIDE is intended to add to the tourist's convenience and pleasure here. It does not purport to be a history. It is a guide book to the St. Augustine of the present.

The illustrations, drawn by MR. ROGER DAVIS, are from his own sketches, made expressly for this work. Their artistic excellence needs no word here. It is a pleasure to add that they have also the merit of rare fidelity to the subjects depicted. They show picturesque St. Augustine—but it is the St. Augustine of actual existence, not a creation of the artist's fancy.

If this little book be not cast aside, its prose and pictures may in the future prove pleasant reminders of a visit to St. Augustine.

DECEMBER 15, 1885.

CONTENTS.

For Ready Reference, - - - - - - 9

The Town, - - - - - - - 12

The Barrier Gateway, - - - - - 26

Fort Marion, - - - - - - - 30

The Plaza, - - - - - - - 51

The Cathedral, - - - - - - 57

The Seawall, - - - - - - - 60

St. Francis Barracks, - - - - - 64

Military Cemetery, - - - - - - 65

The Harbor, - - - - - - - 68

St. Anastasia Island, - - - - - 72

Coquina, - - - - - - - 78

Matanzas, - - - - - - - 78

Floral Calendar, - - - - - - 81

Historical, - - - - - - - 85

OLD HOUSE ON MARINE STREET.

ILLUSTRATIONS

From Drawings by Roger Davis.

		PAGE
RUINS OF GATEWAY, FROM WITHOUT (Frontispiece).		
OLD HOUSE ON MARINE STREET,	- - - - - -	6
ST. GEORGE STREET, LOOKING NORTH,	- - - -	13
ST. GEORGE STREET, LOOKING TOWARD GATEWAY,	- - -	15
DATE PALM, ST. FRANCIS STREET,	- - - - -	17
TREASURY STREET, LOOKING EAST,	- - -	18
TREASURY STREET, LOOKING WEST,	- - - -	19
RUINS OF THE KING'S FORGE,	- - - - -	20
OLD HOUSE, CHARLOTTE STREET,	- -	21
CHARLOTTE STREET,	- - - - - - -	23
VILLA ZORAYDA, KING STREET,	- - - - -	25
RUINS OF GATEWAY, FROM WITHIN,	- -	27
RUINS OF GATEWAY, FROM THE NORTHWEST,	- - -	29
FORT MARION, FROM THE WATER BATTERY,	- -	31
" " ESCUTCHEON,	- - - -	33
" " A CASEMATE DOOR,	- - -	35
" INCLINED PLANE,	- - - -	37
" " NICHE IN CHAPEL,	- - - - -	38
" " SALLY-PORT AND WATCH-TOWER,	- - -	39
" " SOUTHWEST BASTION,	- - -	41
" " FROM SOUTHWEST,	- - -	43
" " SOUTHEAST TOWER,	- - - -	44

Fort Marion, Northeast Tower,   -   -
"   "   Moat and Water Battery,   -
"   "   From the North,   -   -
"   "   Cannon, Northwest **Glacis**,   -
Plaza, Looking Northwest,   -   -
Old Market,   -   -   -   -   -   -
St. George Street and Plaza,
Cathedral,   -   -   -   -
Plaza Basin,   -   -   -   -
Marine Street and **Seawall**,   -   -   -
St. Francis Barracks,   -   -   -
Tombs, Military Cemetery,   -   -
Shore **of** St. Anastasia Island,   -
St. Augustine Light,   -   -   -
Old Lighthouse,   -   -   -
Ruins of **Old** Lighthouse,   -   -
Ruins of **Fort** at Matanzas,   -   -
Date Palm,   -   -   -   -   -
Blossom **of** the Banana,   -   -
End Piece,   -   -   -   -   -

Other Illustrations.

Plan of City and Vicinity,   -   -
Outline of Fort Marion,   -   -   -
Plan of Fort Marion, **from "Old St. Augustine**,
Portrait of Osceola,   -   -   -
Portrait **of** Coacoochee,   -   -
Plan of Plaza,   -   -   -   -
River of Dolphins, from "Old **St.** Augustine."

FOR READY REFERENCE.

APPROACH. From Jacksonville, via Jacksonville, St. Augustine & Halifax River Ry., 36 miles, 2 hours, fare $1.75, excursion $3. From Tocoi (connections with river steamers), via St. Johns Ry., 15 miles, 40 minutes, fare 90 cents, excursion $1.50. Conveyance from depots to any part of town, 25 cents; baggage, 25 cents per piece. Steamboat direct from Jacksonville and New Smyrna. Schedule at this date undetermined.

HOTELS. On the American plan. Rates per day are subjoined, for rates per week and longer periods address proprietors.

Florida House (Geo L. Atkins & Sons), St. George and Treasury streets, 200 guests, $4 per day.

Hotel **San Marco** (O. D. Seavey), Shell Road, near City Gateway, 500 guests, $4.50 per day.

Magnolia **Hotel** (W. W. Palmer), St. George street, 250 guests, $4 per day.

St. Augustine **Hotel** (E. E. Vail), Charlotte street and Plaza, 250 guests, $4 per day.

BOARDING HOUSES. Rates, $1.50 to $3 per day, $8 to $21 per week; number of guests given in parentheses: Edwards House, J. T. Edwards, Charlotte street (75). Ocean View, W. S. M. Pinkham, Bay street (65). Sunnyside, King and Tolomato streets. G. S. Greeno's, Marine street (50). Seaside House, H. Taylor & Co., Bridge street (30). Mrs. M. Frazer's, St. Francis street (25). Baya House, Mrs. E. C. Jouret, Marine and Baya streets (25). Mrs. J. D. Hernandez's, Charlotte street (25). Mrs. Craddock's, Bridge street (20). American House, S. Woodall, Orange street (20). H. H. Neligan's, St. George street (15). Cleveland House, A. M Blake, St. George street (75). Rolleston House, J. T. Scott, St. George street (60). Bay Cottage, J. J. Hamon, Marine street (25). Some of the houses, as the Palm Villa, St. George street and Plaza, and Mrs. Hazeltine's are understood to be filled with permanent guests. Furnished apartments without board: The Villula, J. Brainard, King street (40). Mrs. H. Darling's, Charlotte street (20). Philadelphia House, Mrs. H. J. Pennington, Talomato street. Gordon Block, Mrs. S. V. Simmons (10). Hamblen Block, C. F. Hamblen (20).

RAILWAYS. Jacksonville, St. Augustine & Halifax River Railway (depot on Orange street, north end of town, rear Hotel San Marco), direct to Jacksonville. St. Johns Railway (depot beyond St. Sebastian River, west of town), to Tocoi, on the St. John's River. Through tickets sold from St. Augustine to all points North and West. General ticket offices: Ballard's, on St. George street near Plaza; and Hotel San Marco.

TIME. Standard (railroad) time is 34 minutes slower than local (cathedral) time. Standard time at Ballard's, on St. George street. Persons leaving town should insist on being taken to depot only in proper season for train, otherwise they may be rushed out there an hour ahead of time and left to amuse themselves while the thrifty driver goes back for more passengers and fares.

MAILS. Post office on St. George street, facing Plaza. Hours: Lock boxes, 6:30 A. M. to 8 P. M.; general delivery, 9 A. M. to 7 P. M. Money orders and registered letters, 9 A. M. to 3 P. M. Wm. W. Dewhurst, postmaster. Mail for guests delivered by hotel carriers. Mail time between St. Augustine and New York, 36 hours; Boston, 36 hours; Chicago, 75 hours. For arrival and departure of mails see schedule posted in office.

TELEGRAPH. Three offices: Hospital street, near Plaza, Hotel San Marco, St. Augustine Hotel. Hours, 8 A. M. to 10 P. M. Rates for 10 words, Jacksonville 25 cents; Philadelphia, New York, Boston, Chicago and St. Louis, $1; New Orleans, 75 cents.

EXPRESS. Southern Express Co., office Hospital street, south of Plaza, W. Crichlow, agent.

BANK. The Bank of St. Augustine, Geo. W. Gibbs, cashier; St. George street, near Plaza; 10 A. M. to 2 P. M.

CHURCHES. Episcopalian—Trinity Church, facing Plaza on the south. Services: Sabbath, 11 A. M , 7:30 P. M. Sabbath school, 3:30 P. M. For other services see bulletin on front of church. Rev. Ed. L. Drown. Rectory adjoining church.

Methodist—King street, one block west of Plaza. Services: Sabbath, 11 A. M. 7:30, P. M. Sabbath school, 9:45 A. M. Friday evening, 7:30. Rev. C. C. McClean; residence, Bronson st.

Presbyterian—St. George street, near Bridge street. Services: Sabbath, 11 A M., 7:30 P. M. in chapel, Tolomato street near King street. Sabbath school, 3:30 P. M. in chapel. Wednesday evening (chapel) 7:30. Rev. S. T. Wilson, D.D.; residence, St. George street, just north of Magnolia Hotel.

Roman Catholic—Cathedral, facing Plaza on the north. Services: Sabbath, 6:30 and 10 A. M., 3 and 4 P. M. Rev. P. J. Lynch; residence adjoining cathedral.

PHYSICIANS. Drs. E. M. Alba (Plaza), L. Alexander (St. George street), A. Anderson, J. R. Gibson (U. S. A. Post), W. Miller (St George street), J. K. Rainey (St. George street), W. F. Shine (Bridge street), F. F Smith (post-office building), D. W. Webb (St. George street).

STORES. There are many shops devoted to the sale of curiosities, fancy work, natural productions, souvenirs, photographic views, etc. The town is well supplied with drygoods, hardware, grocery, jewelry, book and drug stores.

LIVERIES. Saddle horses and vehicles, with or without driver, are for hire.

PUBLIC LIBRARY. St. George street, in post-office building Hours, 10 A M to 1 P.M. (daily except Sunday and Thursday), and 3 to 5 P. M. Non-residents borrow books free of charge, leavin ; a deposit of $2, repaid upon return of book. Miss C. L. Sherman, librarian; 2,000 books.

SCHOOLS. Public school (Hospital street), W. E. Knibloe, principal. St. Augustine School (Shell Road), E. S Drown, principal. St Augustine Academy for Young Ladies, Miss L. S Munday, principal. Convent of the Sisters of St. Joseph (St George street).

STEAM AND SAIL BOATS. Small steam craft ply between wharves and beaches (trip 25 cents), Matanzas Inlet (trip $1) and other points; and may be chartered for excursions. Sailboats with skipper, 50 cents to $1 per hour, $2 to $5 per day. Rowboats are for hire by hour or day.

MUSEUMS. Dr. J Vedder's (Bay street, near St. Augustine Hotel) has living specimens of Florida natural history. Geo H. Chapin's Casino (near Fort Marion) contains a varied collection of curiosities.

NEWSPAPERS. "St Augustine Press," J. D. Whitney. "St. John's Weekly," G. W Dickerson. Jacksonville, Savannah, New York and other papers supplied at the news stores.

YACHT CLUB. St. Augustine Yacht Club; Com., E. A. Douglass, of New York; Sect., R. F. Armstrong. Club house, Seawall and Central Wharf.

SOCIETIES. Masonic, C. E. Gard, Sect A. O. U. W., A. W. Corbitt, Sect. Good Templars, F. H. Gretorex, Sect. Institute of Natural Science meets at Presbyterian parsonage on first and third Tuesdays of month.

BARRACKS. Guard mount on parade in front of barracks; at 9 A. M. dress parade Monday, Wednesday and Friday; on other days, same hour, guard mount; also guard mount daily at sunset. Military band gives concert on parade ground daily (except Sundays) 3:30 to 4:30 P. M., and on the Plaza at 7:30 P. M.

POINTS. St. Augustine, in form of government, is a city; Mayor, John Long, office on Hospital street, south of Plaza Population (permanent residents) 3,000. Latitude 29° 50' 48" N., longitude 81° 11' 20' W. Mean temperature for 1884 as follows: Jan. 52.35, Feb. 61.56, March 65.91, April 64.96, May 73 73, June 73.51, July 81 09, Aug 78.96, Sept 78 18, Oct. 73 92, Nov. 63.63, Dec. 60.36 Average for year, 63 Situation of the town healthful, being almost surrounded by salt water and salt marshes. The dug wells are shallow, water supply chiefly from cisterns and artesian wells 200 to 300 feet deep. Bathing establishments furnish sulphur water (artesian well) and salt water baths.

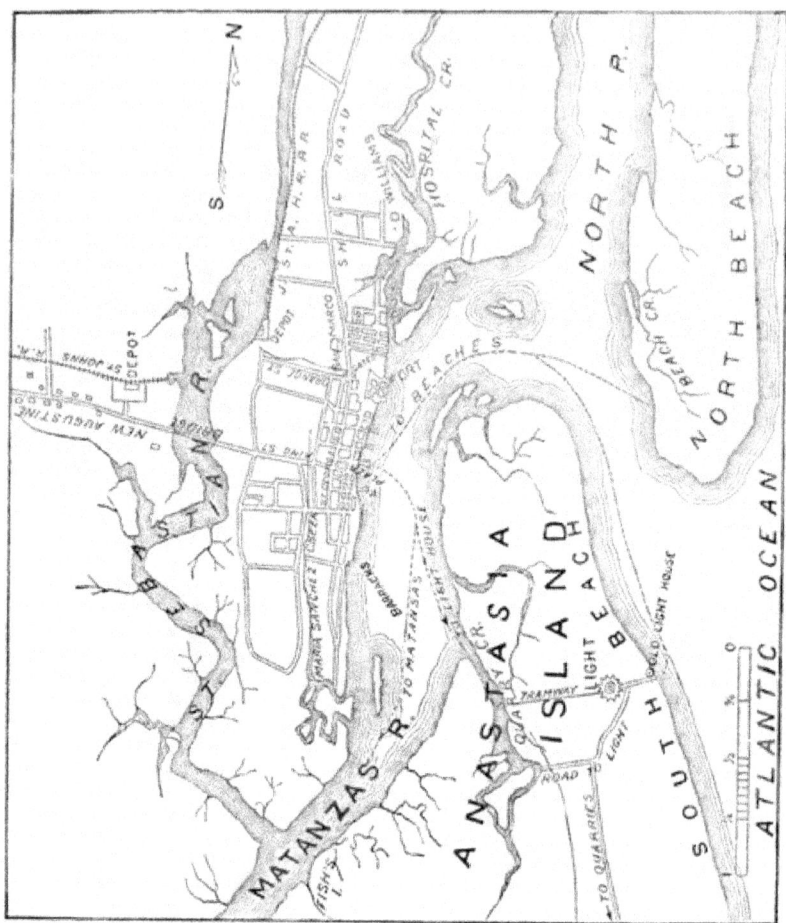

THE TOWN.

FORTIFICATION and defense were the first thought of the Spanish soldiers who founded St. Augustine; and they were careful to choose a site which should be a stronghold. The situation of the town was admirably fitted for such a purpose. St. Augustine is built on a narrow strip of land running north and south. In front, on the east, is the Matanzas River or bay; in the rear (west) the St. Sebastian River, which flows south, then east into the Matanzas. Across the bay, opposite the town, is Anastasia Island; and beyond that, two miles distant, the ocean.

The principal streets run north and south; the cross streets at right angles, east and west. A seawall extends north and south along the water front. At the northern limit of the town are the ruins of the old Barrier Gate, and Fort Marion. At the southern end are the United States barracks. In the centre is an open square or park, called the Plaza.

Historical St. Augustine is bounded by the limits given. The district beyond the city gateway has been built within twenty years, and the quarter below the Barracks within a much more recent period. West of the town, across the St. Sebastian River, is New Augustine.

St George Str.

The town is small. The length from fort to barracks is three-quarters of a mile; width from seawall to St. Sebastian River half a mile. The visitor who is provided with the Standard Guide will need no other aid in finding all points of interest. The statements of drivers and others concerning "the old slave market," "the Huguenot cemetery," "the oldest Spanish house," etc., should be received with a caution amounting to incredulity. The slave market and the Huguenot cemetery do not exist; time spent in searching for them is wasted, sentiment lavished on them is thrown away. They are silly fictions, invented to sell guide books, and to coax "tips" from tourists. The cemetery near the city gate is not a Huguenot cemetery. The Huguenots were not buried there. There were no Huguenots in St. Augustine. It is not certainly known which is the oldest Spanish house.

There is very much in St. Augustine which is of genuine interest, whether one's stay here be short or long. The principal points to be seen are :

> THE RUINS OF THE GATE.
> FORT MARION.
> PLAZA AND SURROUNDINGS.

These may most conveniently be visited in the order given. The Fort is the most important, and as much time should be reserved for that as for all the others combined. Then there are the seawall, the barracks and the military cemetery, the narrow streets—such as have not lost their picturesqueness—and numerous excursions by land and water to various points named elsewhere.

The principal street is St. George, extending north and south through the centre of the town. On this street are the Presbyterian Church, Post Office, Florida House, Magnolia Hotel and City Gateway. The Shell Road which passes the Hotel San Marco is a continuation of St. George street. West of St. George, and parallel with it, is Tolomato. East, and parallel, is Charlotte. Marine street is on the water front, north of the Plaza; Bay street on the water front south of the Plaza.

ST. GEORGE STREET.

St. Francis street, at the southern end of the town, is famous for the overhanging date palm tree which has so often been pictured. Another well-known street is the narrow lane called Treasury street, across which, with back to opposite wall, two persons may readily grasp hands.

Some of these street names are suggestive of incidents in the town's romantic history. St. Francis commemorates the labors and self sacrifice of the Franciscan mission fathers, whose monastic institution was on the site where the barracks now stand. Tolomato perpetuates the name of the Indian village where, in 1597, certain of these Franciscans were heartlessly massacred by their rebellious flocks. Cuna and St. Hypolita were given in the Spanish supremacy. St. George street was so called in honor of England's patron saint, and Charlotte was the name of the queen of King George IV. "Old St. Augustine" states that the name Treasury is from the Spanish term, which signified "the street where the treasurer lives." The treasure (*i. c.*, funds for the soldiers' pay, etc. was kept closely guarded in the fort. It is told of the Spanish treasurer that he began to build a house without first counting the cost. This was on the corner of what are now St. George and Treasury streets. The elaborately entablatured walls of this great mansion were only partially finished when Florida was ceded to the United States, and the treasurer, with all the other of the King's s.rvants, abandoned St. Augustine. The ruins of these walls were still standing until supplanted by the picket fence of the Florida House yard.

The narrow little streets, with their foreign names and foreign throngs, their overhanging balconies and high garden walls, through whose open door one caught a glimpse of orange and fig and waving banana, were among the quaint characteristics which made this old Florida town charming and peculiar among all American cities But the picturesque streets, of which tourists have so often written, have almost ceased to be a pleasing feature of St. Augustine. Some are widened. Others, changed past all recognition and shorn of their quaintness, are inconvenient and quite inadequate to meet the

DATE PALM, ST. FRANCIS STREET.

TREASURY STREET — LOOKING EAST.

TREASURY STREET — LOOKING WEST.

Blacksmith Shop

RUINS OF THE KING'S FORGE.

demands of the time. One can hardly blame the ill-starred pedestrian crowded to the wall by reckless jehus, and mud-bespattered by the flying wheels—if he sigh for the good old times when, tradition has it, no vehicle was allowed on the concrete-paved streets of Spanish St. Augustine.

OLD HOUSE ON CHARLOTTE STREET.

Few of the dwellings are remarkable for antiquity or peculiarity of construction; their picturesque side is usually the exterior, and may be seen from the street. On Hospital street, just south of the Plaza, stands an old house whose arched corridor has been frequently illustrated; but instead of visiting this relic of old times, one will do well to content himself with the photographs which are for sale at the shops, for the pretty scene they picture no longer exists. The corridor has done duty as a storage for hardware, and its beauty has long since departed.

The style of architecture is undergoing a change; one by one the overhanging balconies are disappearing from the streets. High walls are replaced by picket fences and wire netting. Moss-roofed houses have given way to smart shops. Lattice gates are displaced by show windows, and displays of bargains in ready-made clothing. For an example of this innovation, compare the smart business row on St. George street near the Plaza with the same street (see illustration page 56, as it was fifteen years ago. And how long will it be before the other old houses and walls shown in these pages will have shared the same fate?

In former times, most of the houses were of coquina (a loose shell-stone, quarried on the island opposite), but this material is now almost entirely superseded by wood. Roomy and modern wooden houses may not be so picturesque as the weather-stained coquina dwellings they have supplanted, but they are immeasurably more comfortable to live in.

The people met in the streets are not the picturesque beings one may find described in the books of travel written fifty years ago. Many strangers expect to find a Spanish population. They have a notion—zealously fostered by the stereotyped " Ancient City " letter in Northern newspapers—that inasmuch as St. Augustine was founded by the Spaniards there must be Spaniards here now. As a matter of fact, the swarthy Spaniard stalks through the streets no longer, save in the mushy imagination of feminine correspondents, who send gushing screeds to distant newspapers. The Spanish residents

CHARLOTTE STREET.

emigrated when Florida was ceded to the United States seventy-four years ago. The Minorcans (a colony from Minorca in the Mediterranean Sea) remained here after the change of flags; but even they are now an inconspicuous part of the winter throngs that fill the streets.

So in one way and another the town has taken on new appearance and character. From a queerly built old city, whose foreign air piqued the curiosity of the chance visitor, and hinted of the strange vicissitudes of its three centuries, St. Augustine has become a fashionable winter resort, whose great hotels dominate the aspect of town and country round about; and whose visitors in "the rush" outnumber the permanent residents. The Newport of the South they call it now.

And yet, with all its innovations and transformations the town has not lost its attractions. It still maintains a distinctive character all its own; and there is still about the old city an indefinable charm which leads one's thoughts back to it again, and gladdens the face that is once more turned toward Florida and St. Augustine.

On King street, near Bronson, is the Villa Zorayda, the winter residence of Franklin W. Smith, Esq., of Boston. This is notable for its architectural design and the elaborate manner in which its owner-architect has successfully developed his plan of an oriental building as appropriate to the latitude of Florida—the conception having been borrowed from the universal practice of Eastern countries, demonstrating the experience of centuries. The architecture throughout is strictly Moorish, after sketches and photographs in Spain, Tangiers and Algiers. Like the Alhambra itself, the Zorayda is of massive concrete. The walls have the external appearance of granite, with all of its durability. Above the front entrance is the inscription in Arabic letters: *Wa la ghalib illa-llah*—There is no conqueror but God. This is the motto everywhere reproduced on the escutcheons and in the tracery of the Alhambra. The tradition is that a Moorish king, returning from an exploit, was greeted at the gate by the shouts of the populace and hailed as the conqueror, but

raising his hand he exclaimed, "There is no conqueror but God."
Within the walls of the Zorayda is a central court, paved with tiles
made for it in Spain, and surrounded by a double gallery supported
on thirty-six horseshoe arches.   The walls of the vestibule, court and
drawing-room are covered with the moresque tracery of the Alhambra, the models having been imported for the purpose.   In this
detail of construction and ornamentation the Zorayda is the first
illustration in the United States.   The interior finish, furniture and
ornaments richly illustrate the beauties of Moorish colors and forms,
and the pleasing effect is heightened by the tropical foliage and
fruits in the protected court.

VILLA ZORAYDA.

THE BARRIER GATEWAY.

*At the head of St. George Street, on Orange Street, mid-
way between the Fort and the Railway Depot.*

LANDMARKS are rapidly disappearing from St.
Augustine, but the pillars of the city gateway
still remain as notable monuments of the past.
The first view of them is likely to be a disap-
pointment. The gateway has been outgrown
and dwarfed. It no longer possesses even the advantage of a
commanding position on the town's outskirts. Dwellings crowd
close upon it, overtopping the towers; a huge hotel looms up beyond.
Irreverence might even dub the gate ridiculous.

But it was not always so. Inconsequential as are these towers
to-day, there was a time when they stood out bravely enough, and
when in their security St. Augustine rejoiced. In those days they
looked out upon an illimitable wilderness. The belated traveler
hurried on to their shelter. The town slept securely when the
Barrier Gate was fast shut against the midnight enemy. Stoutly
these walls gave their strength when it was needed, and defended
for the King of Spain his garrison town in Florida. They have wit-
nessed many a narrow escape and many a gallant rescue. More

RUINS OF GATEWAY—FROM WITHIN.

than once have they trembled with the shock of assault, and more than once driven back the foe repulsed. To-day, dismantled and useless, out of accord with the customs of the day and the spirit of the age, and long since left behind by the outstretching town, the picturesque old ruins linger as cherished landmarks. Here we are on historic ground.

The gateway is the only conspicuous relic of the elaborate system of fortifications which once defended the town. The advantages of St. Augustine's position for such defense already has been alluded to. The town is built on a narrow peninsula running south; and an enemy could approach by land only from the north. Across this northern boundary, east to west, from water to water, ran lines of fortification, which effectually barred approach. From the Fort a deep ditch ran across to the St. Sebastian. This was defended by a high parapet, redoubts and batteries. The ditch was flooded at high tide. Entrance to the town was by a drawbridge across this moat and through the gate. The Fort defended the harbor. Earthworks extended along the St. Sebastian River back west of the town, and around to the Matanzas again on the south. The gate was closed at night. Guards were stationed in the sentry boxes. A guard house, with a detachment of troops, was just within the gate. The line of the ditch and parapet may still be traced along Orange street; and the remains of some of the old earthworks are to be seen along the St. Sebastian.

The towers are very old. They had fallen into partial ruin so early as the beginning of the present century. In 1810, at the Governor's command, all the town's male inhabitants between 12 and 60 years of age were compelled to labor at the restoration of the gate and the other fortifications. Men are still living here who remember this enforced service. At a later date the west tower was partially demolished and then clumsily rebuilt. The stone causeway leading out from the gate is modern. The sentry boxes have recently been repaired and are now furnished with iron gratings to protect them from the vandals who know no better than to chip off pieces of stone as relics. The material is coquina. The pillars are 20 feet in height, to the mouldings; and 10 feet deep; the flanking walls are 30 feet in length; the roadway between the pillars, 12 feet. The walls were formerly provided with banquettes, or raised platforms on the interior, upon which the guard stepped to discharge his fire over the wall, with a single step regaining shelter.

RUINS OF GATEWAY—FROM THE NORTHWEST.

FORT MARION.

FORT MARION is at the north end of the city and commands the harbor. It is not occupied by troops. Open daily (admission free) from 8 A. M. to 4 P. M. For a visit the afternoon is the most pleasant time. Sergeant George M. Brown, who is in charge, will conduct visitors through the casemates. For this service, which is voluntary, a fee (not demanded) is usually given.

The fort, which is the only example of mediæval fortification on this continent, is a magnificent specimen of the art of military engineering as developed at the time of its construction. It is a massive structure of coquina stone, with curtains, bastions, moat and outworks, covering an acre. The following description of the fort is based on that given in "Old St. Augustine," from which volume the plan (page 34) is borrowed.

Surrounding the fort on the three land sides is an immense artificial hill of earth, called the *glacis*. From the crest of the glacis on the southeast, a bridge (1), formerly a drawbridge, leads across part of the moat to the barbacan. The *barbacan* is a fortification, surrounded by the moat, directly in front of the fort

FORT MARION — FROM THE WATER BATTERY.

entrance, which it was designed to protect. In the barbacan at the stairway 2 are the Arms of Spain. A second bridge (3', originally a drawbridge, leads from the barbacan across the wide *moat* to the *sally-port* (4 , which is the sole entrance to the fort. This was provided with a heavy door called the *portcullis*. On the outer wall, above the sally-port is the *escutcheon*, bearing the Arms of Spain; and the Spanish *legend*, which reads:

REYNANDO EN ESPANA EL SEN^R
DON FERNANDO SEXTO Y SIENDO
GOV^{OR} Y CAP^N DE ESA C^D S^{AN} AUG^N DE
LA FLORIDA E SUS PROV^A EL MARESCAL
DE CAMPO D^NALONZO FERN^{DO} HEREDA ,
ASI CONCLUIO ESTE CASTILLO EL AN
OD 1756 DIRI^CENDO LAS OBRAS EL
CAP INGN^{RO} DN PEDRO DE BROZAS
Y GARAY

Translation: " Don Ferdinand VI., being King of Spain, and the Field Marshal Don Alonzo Fernando Hereda being Governor and Captain-General of this place, San Augustin of Florida, and its province, this fort was finished in the year 1756. The works were directed by the Captain-Engineer, Don Pedro de Brozas of Garay."

The inscription has been almost obliterated by the elements. Its present condition is shown in the illustration opposite.

Within the fort, on the right of the entrance hall 5 is the old bake room (6), and beyond this are two dark chambers 7 and 8 ,

OUTLINE OF FORT MARION.
A, covered way. B, bastion. C, curtain. G, glacis. M, moat. T, watch-tower. W, water battery.

FORT MARION — ESCUTCHEON.

which were probably used for storage. On the left is the guards'
room 7 left. The hall opens upon a large square court 103 by
109 feet. Around this court are *casemates* 10, or rooms which
were used for barracks, messrooms, storage, etc. Some of these
casemates were divided into lower and upper apartments. To each
west casemate a beam of light is admitted through a narrow window or *embrasure*, high up near the arched ceiling. From the first
east casemate a door leads back into an interior dark room 9).
From the furthest casemate 11 on the same side an entrance leads

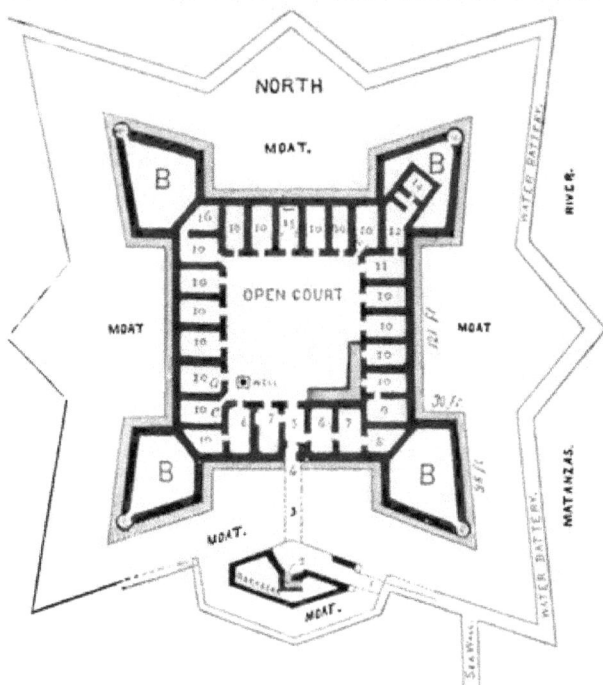

PLAN OF FORT MARION.

1, bridge from barbacan to glacis. 2, stairway of barbacan. 3, bridge over moat. 4, sally-port.
5, hall. 6, bake room. 7, 8, dark rooms. 7 (left), guards' room. 6 (left), officers' room. 9, interior dark room. 10, 10, casemates. 11, casemate. 12, interior dark room. 14, bomb proof. 15,
chapel. 16, dark room. 10a, treasurer's room. 10c, casemate from which Coacoochee escaped
B, bastion. W, watch-tower.

FORT MARION — A CASEMATE DOOR.

back into a dark chamber 12, off from which a narrow passage leads through a wall 5 feet deep into a space 5 feet wide; and from this a low aperture 2 feet square gives access through another wall 5 feet deep, into an innermost tomb-like chamber 14 which is 19½ feet long, 13²³ feet broad, and 8 feet high. The arched roof is of solid masonry. This dungeon-like room has no other outlet than the single low aperture. It was probably designed for a powder magazine or a bomb-proof. When the fort was in perfect repair the chamber may have been dry and fit for use as a safe deposit for explosives, but afterward, when the water from above percolated through the coquina, this bomb-proof or powder magazine must have become damp and unwholesome. For this reason it was no longer used except as a place to throw rubbish into. Then it bred fevers; and finally, as a sanitary measure, the Spaniards walled it up. The entrance from the outer or middle room 12 was closed with masonry. It was so shut when the United States came into possession of the fort; and the existence of these inner chambers was not suspected until in 1839, while the engineers were making some repairs, the closed entrance was noticed; and investigation led to the discovery of the interior passageways. Refuse and rubbish were found there. The report was given out—whether at the time or later—that in this rubbish were some bones. From this insignificant beginning the myth-makers evolved first the tale that the bones were human; then they made them a complete skeleton; then two skeletons; then they added a rusty chain and a staple in the wall—a gold ring on one skeleton's finger—instruments of torture—two iron cages—and when Charles Lanman visited the fort in 1850, they had supplied one of the skeletons with a pair of boots—and showed the boots to prove the gold ring, staples, iron cages, and all the other stock accessories to the Spanish Inquisition tale of horror. It was a harmless fiction after all, and that it was not true, more's the pity. However commonplace and practical may have been the use of these underground passages in old times, they are uncanny and mystersious enough now, and

FORT MARION — INCLINED PLANE.

when one follows the guide's torch from the dark rooms into the
last gloomy pent recess, some such tale of luckless victim entombed
alive harmonizes with the flickering torch and dimly seen smoke-
begrimed encompassing walls.

Facing the court on the north was the chapel 15 . Its walls
and ceiling and altar
and niches are bright
with mould and moss
and lichen; strange mu-
tations have come to
town and fort since the
room was dismantled of
its ornaments. The
chapel was used for
religious services as
late as the civil war.
In 1875 it was con-
verted into a school-
room for the Western
Indians who were con-
fined here. The elab-
orate portico of the
chapel was the most
pretentious bit of archi-
tecture in the fort ;
but has so crumbled
away that its form can
no longer be traced. In
the wall outside, above
the chapel door, the
French astronomers,
who came here in 1879

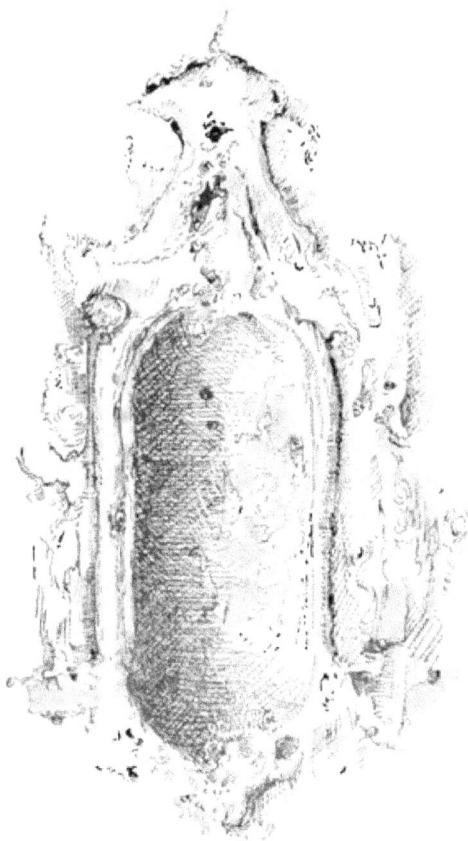

NICHE IN CHAPEL.

to observe the transit of Venus, have left a marble tablet in commemoration of the visit. The inscription reads: " Plaque commem-

Entrance to Fort.

Out out...

Sea Wall.

Fort from Sea Wall.

Lookout from Watch Tower.

FORT MARION — SALLY-PORT AND WATCH TOWER.

orative du passage de Venus observé au Fort Marion le 9 Décembre,
1882, par MM. le Colonel Perrier, le Commandant Bassat, le Capi-
taine Delfoges, de l'Armée Française."

In the northwest bastion is another dark room 16 . Some of the
dark dungeons of the fort
have been used at differ-
ent times for the confine-
ment of prisoners. Patri-
ots from Charleston were
confined here by the British in the Revolution;
the Spaniards kept the
famous outlaw McGirth
in one of these cells five
years; and there are old
people in St. Augustine
to-day who will tell of
pallid convicts led from
the fort dungeons to exe-
cution. At the close of

OSCEOLA.

the last war refractory soldiers were punished by solitary confine-
ment in these cells. Casemate 10c is known as "Coacoochee's
cell;" and is famous as the one from which that chief escaped.
Coacoochee and Osceola, two of the most influential chiefs of the
Seminoles, in the war which began in 1836, were finally captured,
with a number of their followers, and imprisoned in the casemates
at Fort Marion, whence they were to be taken to Fort Moultrie
in Charleston harbor. Coacoochee resolved upon escape. His
subsequent account of the affair was as follows:

"We had been growing sickly from day to day, and so resolved to make our
escape, or die in the attempt. We were in a room, eighteen or twenty feet square.
All the light admitted was through a hole (embrasure), about eighteen feet from
the floor. Through this we must effect our escape, or remain and die with sick-
ness. A sentinel was constantly posted at the door. As we looked at it from
our beds, we thought it small, but believed that, could we get our heads through,

FORT MARION.

SOUTHWEST BASTION NORTHWEST BASTION—BRIDGE TO BARBACAN—ANCIENT CHIMNEY.

we should have no further nor serious difficulty. To reach the hole was the first object. In order to effect this, we from time to time cut up the forage-bags allowed us to sleep on, and made them into ropes. The hole I could not reach when upon the shoulder of my companion; but while standing upon his shoulder, I worked a knife into a crevice of the stonework, as far up as I could reach, and upon this I raised myself to the aperture, when I found that, with some reduction of person, I could get through. In order to reduce ourselves as much as possible, we took medicine five days. Under the pretext of being very sick, we were permitted to obtain the roots we required. For some weeks we watched the moon, in order that the night of our attempt it should be as dark as possible. At the proper time we commenced the medicine, calculating upon the entire disappearance of the moon. The keeper of this prison, on the night determined upon to make the effort, annoyed us by frequently coming into the room, and talking and singing. At first we thought of tying him and putting his head in a bag; so that, should he call for assistance, he could not be heard. We first, however, tried the experiment of pretending to be asleep, and when he returned to pay no regard to him. This accomplished our object. He came in, and went immediately out; and we could hear him snore in the immediate vicinity of the door. I then took the rope, which we had secreted under our

COACOOCHEE.

bed, and mounting upon the shoulder of my comrade, raised myself by the knife worked into the crevices of the stone, and succeeded in reaching the embrasure. Here I made fast the rope, that my friend might follow me. I then passed through the hole a sufficient length of it to reach the ground upon the outside (about twenty-five feet) in the ditch. I had calculated the distance when going for roots. With much difficulty I succeeded in getting my head through; for the sharp stones took the skin off my breast and back. Putting my head through first, I was obliged to go down head foremost, until my feet were through, fearing every moment the rope would break. At last, safely on the ground, I awaited with anxiety the arrival of my comrade. I had passed another rope through the hole, which, in the event of discovery, Talmus Hadjo was to pull, as a signal to me from the outside, that he was discovered, and could not come. As soon as I struck the ground, I took hold of the signal, for intelli-

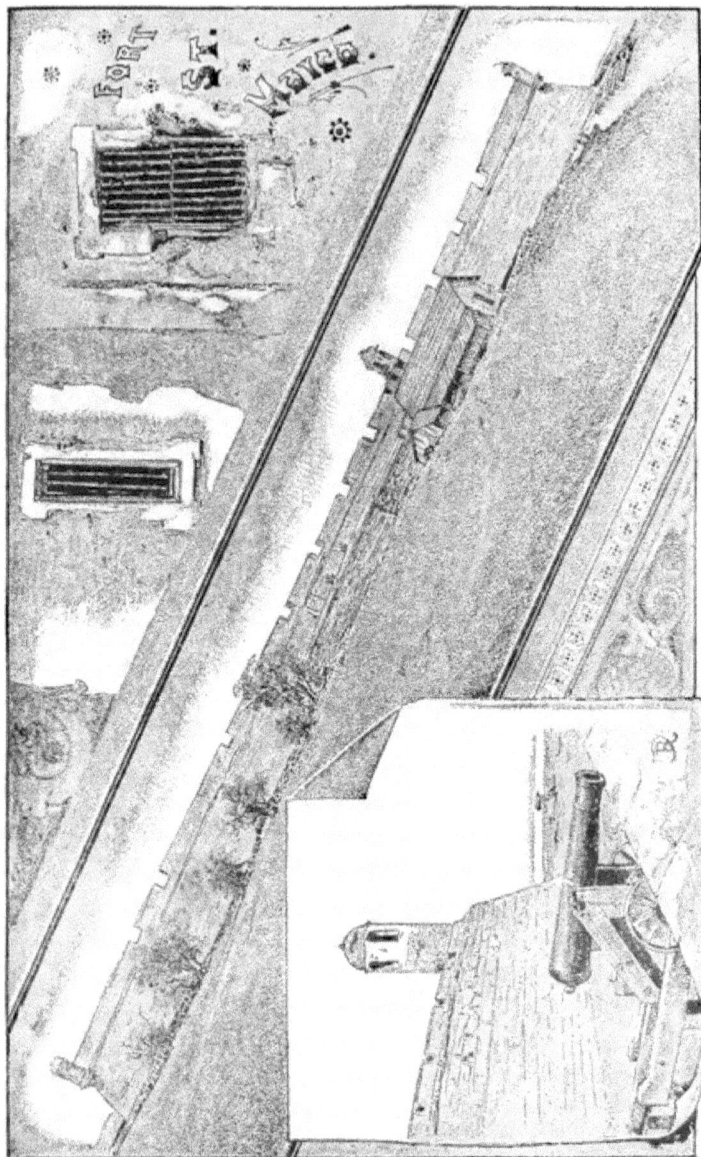

FORT MARION — FROM SOUTHWEST.

FORT MARION — SOUTHEAST TOWER.

FORT MARION — NORTHEAST TOWER.

gence from my friend. The night was very dark. Two men passed near me, talking earnestly, and I could see them distinctly. Soon I heard the struggle of my companion far above me. He had succeeded in getting his head through, but his body would come no farther. In the lowest tone of voice, I urged him to throw out his breath, and then try; soon after, he came tumbling down the whole distance. For a few moments I thought him dead. I dragged him to some water close by, which restored him; but his leg was so lame he was unable to walk. I took him upon my shoulder to a scrub, near the town. Daylight was just breaking, it was evident we must move rapidly. I caught a mule in the adjoining field, and making a bridle out of my sash, mounted my companion, and started for the St. John's River. The mule we used one day, but fearing the whites would track us, we felt more secure on foot in the hammock, though moving very slow. Thus we continued our journey five days, subsisting upon roots and berries, when I joined my band, then assembled on the headwaters of the Tomoka River, near the Atlantic coast."

Coacoochee finally surrendered and was removed to Arkansas, where he took the leadership of his people. Osceola was removed to Fort Moultrie, where shortly after he died.

From the southeast of the court, to the right of the entrance hall, an inclined plane of stonework leads up to the platform *(terreplein)* of the ramparts. The original inclined plane is to be replaced by a new one.

At the outer angle of each *bastion B* is a sentry box W, that on the northwest 25 feet high being also a watch-tower for looking to seaward. A stroke of lightning shattered the sentry-box on the northwest corner. Distance from corner to corner, 317 feet. The four sides of the fort between the bastions are the *curtains.* There are four equal bastions and four equal curtains. The walls of bastions and curtains are 9 feet thick at base, 4½ at top, and 25 feet high, above the present moat level. Battlements similar to those on the other sides formerly defended the east water) side of the ramparts. The bastions are filled with earth, and there is no foundation for the romantic tale of a subterranean passageway from the southwest bastion to a neighboring convent.

The moat is 40 feet wide. It was formerly deeper than at present, had a perfectly cemented concrete floor, and was flooded at high tide. The excavation of the moat of San Marco is an

FORT MARION — MOAT AND WATER BATTERY.

archæological task waiting to richly reward some enthusiastic St. Augustine Schliemann.

Running along the outer edge of the moat are narrow level spaces called *covered-ways;* and wider levels called *places-of-arms,* where artillery was mounted and the troops gathered, protected by the outer wall or *parapet,* from which slopes the glacis.

The fortification of stone water battery) in front is of modern construction, having been built by the United States in 1842; and the small brick building (hot shot furnace) in the moat between the east curtain and the water battery dates from 1844. The guns of the battery have been dismounted, and all but one or two removed.

In different forms and bearing different names, St. Augustine's fort has been established more than three centuries; for two hundred years the fort was St. Augustine, and St. Augustine was Florida. First a rude and temporary fortification of logs, it expanded in plan and magnitude until developed into the great stone fortress of 1756. Menendez utilized the Indian council house as a defense against the Huguenots from Fort Caroline. After his massacre of the French at Matanzas Inlet, the Spaniard stood in just fear of a hostile fleet from France; and he set about the building of a regular fort of logs. Twenty years later Francis Drake took this fort—San Juan de Pinos —and destroyed it; when the Spaniards, having discovered the coquina quarries on Anastasia Island, undertook the construction of a fort of stone. In those days the progress of such a work was slow; and when the Boucaniers came in 1665, the fort, though well under way, was not in a condition to offer any resistance. Convicts from Spain and Mexico, Indians and slaves, toiled at the walls; and when Jonathan Dickenson, the shipwrecked Philadelphia Quaker, came to St. Augustine in 1695, he found the fort, curtain and bastion walls thirty feet high. This was the fort San Marco, which Moore of Carolina fruitlessly besieged in 1712, and Oglethorpe of Georgia cannonaded without effect for forty days in 1740. Fort San Marco was one of a series of works defending St. Augustine; other forts were north of the town, on the St. Johns River, and at Matanzas.

FORT MARION — FROM THE NORTH.

Shortly after coming into the possession of the United States, the Fort was named Fort Marion, in honor of the famous Revolutionary partisan, General Francis Marion.

The Fort is built of coquina, which in its day was considered a very excellent material for this purpose, since cannon balls would sink into the wall without shattering it as they would harder stone. On the sea front of the southwest bastion are a number of crevices which, according to local tradition, were caused by British cannon balls from the opposite shore. In those days of crude weapons, the coquina bastions were capable of withstanding a much harder attack than Oglethorpe's; but the art of war has changed since that time, and Fort Marion's coquina would succumb to artillery of the present.

The Fort has been dismantled. A few antiquated and long-silent cannon are preserved as suggestions of the warlike character of the surroundings, and here and there the rusted throat of a half buried gun breaks the surface of the moat; while on the northwest crest of the glacis reposes a great cannon, about which cattle peacefully browse and children innocently play.

CANNON ON NORTHWEST GLACIS.

THE PLAZA.

TRANSFORMATION has been wrought in the little public square in the centre of the town. It is now a beautiful park of shrubbery and shade trees, with monuments and fountains, an antiquated market place inviting one to loiter, and an outlook to the east over the bay and Anastasia Island to the sails of ships at sea. All this is the more charming to those who remember the Plaza — not so many years ago — when it was a shadeless, unkempt, uninviting waste of scanty turf and blowing sand. Long before those days it had been beautiful with orange trees, whose wonderful size and fruitfulness are yet among the town's traditions. The square is diminutive, but it is unconciously magnified and dignified because of the contrast to the narrow streets whence one emerges upon its stretch of greensward.

It takes its name from the monument erected here by the Spaniards in 1813. This is a pyramid of coquina, stuccoed and whitewashed, rising from a stone pedestal, and surmounted by a cannon ball. It is not a work of high artistic pretension, nor of very imposing proportions, but its history is curious. The existence of such a memorial here in the United States is incongruous, for it commemorates a minor event of European history.

PLAZA — LOOKING NORTHWEST.

"Charles IV. having been compelled to abdicate the Spanish throne in favor of Ferdinand VII., Napoleon Bonaparte was called to arbitrate between them. He extorted from both a resignation of their claims, and placed his own brother, Joseph Napoleon, on the throne 1808. An insurrection of the Spanish people followed. The French troops were employed to support Napoleon, and England, recognizing the claims of Ferdinand VII., aided the cause of the insurgents. In 1812, the Spanish Cortes the legislative body representing the insurgents) completed the formation of a new and liberal constitution. In commemoration of this, monuments were erected in Spain and the Spanish provinces. Among others was this one in the province of Florida, the square then taking the name *Plaza de la Constitucion.* Finally, in 1814, the war for independence was brought to a successful termination; and Ferdinand VII., having pledged himself to support the new constitution, was recalled to the throne. Once in power, almost his first act was to repudiate the new constitution and declare it null and void. Throughout Spain and her American dependencies it was commanded that the monuments erected two years previously in commemoration of the constitution, should be destroyed. Notwithstanding the royal decree, this one in Florida was not torn down. The tablets were removed, but four years later 1818 were restored to their places, where they have remained ever since."— *Old St. Augustine, p.* 121

In each of three sides is set a marble tablet, bearing the inscription *Plaza de la Constitucion*; and on the east side graven in delightfully antiquated characters is the following inscription:

PLAZA DE LA CONSTITUCION.

PROMULGADA EN ESTA CIUDAD DE SAN
AGUSTIN DE LA FLORIDA ORIENTAL EN
17 DE OCTUBRE DE 1812 SIENDO GOBERNO
DOR EL BRIGADIER DON SEBASTIAN KIN
DALEM CABALLERO DEL ORDEN DE SANTIAGO

PEIRA ETERNA MEMORIA.

EL AYUNTAMIENTO CONSTITUCIONAL ERIGIO
ESTE OBELISCO DIRIGIDO POR DON FERNANDO
DE LA PLAZA ARREDONDO EL JOVEN REGIDOR
DECANO Y DON FRANCISCO ROBIRA
PROCURADOR SINDICO.—

AÑO DE 1813.

The translation is : " Plaza of the Constitution, promulgated in the city of St. Augustine, in East Florida, on the 17th day of October, in the year 1812; the Brigadier Don Sebastian Kindalem, Knight of the Order of Santiago, being Governor. For eternal remembrance the Constitutional City Council erected this monument, under the superintendence of Don Fernando de la Maza Arredondo, the young municipal officer, oldest member of the corporation, and Don Francisco Robira, Attorney and Recorder. In the year 1813."

A Mason'c emblem, beneath the legend, is no part of the original

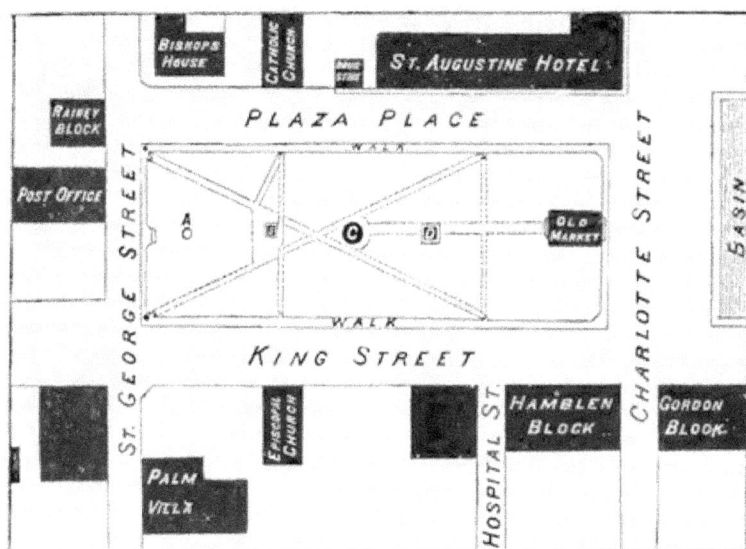

A, C, FOUNTAINS. B, PLAZA MONUMENT. D, CONFEDERATE MONUMENT.

design; it was cut recently, and is of the nature of a disfigurement.
Don Fernando de la Maza Arredondo was a wealthy merchant.
It has been stated, though on no sufficient authority, that this is the
only monument of the sort now in existence.

A second monument in the Plaza, erected in 1879 by the Ladies'
Memorial Association, is to commemorate the volunteers from St.
Augustine and vicinity, who lost their lives in the Confederate
service. The shaft is of coquina, and bears the inscriptions:

Our Dead. Erected by the Ladies' Memorial Association of St. Augustine. Fla., A. D. 1872.

In Memoriam. Our loved ones who gave their lives in the armre of the Confederate States.

They died far from the home that gave them birth.

They have crossed the river and rest under the shade of the trees.

The open structure on the east end of the Plaza was built in 1840

for a public market. It is erroneously said to be of Spanish origin,
but the Spaniards had left St. Augustine twenty years previous to its
building. Since the last war, it has done duty as a slave market.
Before that time, it was a very ordinary, unpretentious commonplace depot for the sale of meat and fish, to secure his daily portion of which the St. Augustine householder repaired to the Plaza
market in the darkness of early morning or on Saturday afternoons
—weekly occasions of unwonted bustle in the quiet town. The re-
quirements of St. Augustine have long outgrown this primitive style
of marketing, and the old mart has been turned into a lounging-
place, where citizen and stranger meet to bask in the sunshine and
drink sulphur water. At stated intervals the military band uses this

THE OLD MARKET.

ST. GEORGE STREET AND PLAZA.

as a music stand for the benefit of the St. Augustine Hotel guests in particular, and the whole town in general.

The fountains are supplied by the flow of artesian wells; and the water is strongly impregnated with sulphur. If allowed to stand in the open air, the sulphur taste and odor disappear.

Always a place of public assembly, the Plaza has been the scene of two incidents which strikingly illustrate the curious vicissitudes of the town's history. The first of these was on that historic night in the year 1776 when the British subjects of King George IV. assembled here and burned in effigy two of the signers of the Declaration of Independence; and the second, a hundred years later, was the Fourth of July gathering of St. Augustine in mass meeting on the Plaza to applaud the reading of that Declaration.

Originally, no doubt, the square was designed as a parade for the maneuvering of troops. On a map of the town in British times, as given in " Old St. Augustine," it is called " The Parade Ground." For this it was employed so late as the close of the civil war, when the sunset dress-parade of the United States troops on the Plaza was—next to the daily arrival of the mail stage—the great event of the day. A person of antiquarian tastes might find much of interest in the alterations which have been made during the last fifty years in the Plaza surroundings. King street, the broad, shaded street which runs west, was originally a high-walled alley ten feet wide; another wall shut in the lot where the Post Office stands, on the site of the old Governor's house, and another extended from St. George street south to the Cathedral, and then to Charlotte street, where on the corner stood the guard house—the site of the St. Augustine Hotel.

Facing the Plaza on the west St. George street is the Post Office; the east is open to the bay. On the south rises the spire of Trinity Church; and on the north (west of the St. Augustine Hotel is

THE CATHEDRAL.

Before the era of winter hotels in St. Augustine, the Cathedral was the most imposing structure between Fort and Barracks; and, though somewhat overshadowed by the great caravansary near by, it still remains the most interesting of the Plaza's surroundings. In architecture the edifice is of Colonial fashion, with classic and Queen Anne features intermingled. The entrance is through a door with full-centred arched top, and is flanked on either side by double columns of severe type, supporting a heavy pediment. On either side in the blank wall are small windows with arched top; while above, close under the cornice line, are small, round windows of a Dutch pattern. In the gable, above the projecting cornice, which is carried across the street façade and rests on broad pilasters at either angle, is a small window with a " sunburst," surmounting what is now a clock but was formerly a mural sun-dial. Instead of following the rigid line of the roof rafters, the front wall is finished off at the sides in an ogee curve, while above a mask wall is carried up as a belfry. This is

lightened in appearance by three arched window openings, above
the ridge line of the roof. Each of these fenestral openings has
been utilized for the hanging of a bell, while a fourth bell is in yet
another similar opening above. A curious feature is the open corridor running along behind the wall for the accommodation of the
bell-ringers. A ball is set upon the apex of the wall, attached to
this is a vane, and surmounting all rises the Latin cross.

Within the Cathedral, on the left of the vestibule, is a silver cruci-
fix, which formerly belonged to an older church—*Nostra Senora
de la Leche*, which was torn down, and its ornaments sold for the
construction of the present Cathedral. The interior of the church
is, like the exterior, of severe type. Among the paintings is one of
recent production and indifferent merit, which has for its historical
subject "The First Mass in St. Augustine."

Of the four bells, three are rung or jangled in a way quite peculiar to the town. One of these bells, that in the west niche, is a
beautiful piece of artistic workmanship. It bears the inscription:
" Sancte · Joseph · Ora · Pro · Nobis · D · 1682." It has been
claimed for this bell that it is the oldest on this Continent; it may
be the most ancient within the limits of the United States, antedating
by three years the famous bell in the Dutch church at Tarrytown,
N. Y., which bears the date 1685. The Cathedral itself is not old
when compared with some other church edifices in this country; it
is, for example, nearly a hundred years more modern than the Tarrytown church just referred to. It was completed in 1791. The
material is coquina, which is stuccoed. The church is open during
the day; admission to the belfry is by special permit.

THE CATHEDRAL.

THE SEAWALL.

XTENDING from the water-battery of Fort Marion south along the water front of the town to the United States barracks, stands a seawall of coquina capped with New England granite. It affords a necessary protection against the encroachment of the sea. The site of St.Augustine is so low that under certain conditions of wind and tide the waves would inundate much of the town, and the damage would be irreparable. As it is, in heavy east storms the water dashes over the top of the wall and sometimes floods the adjacent streets.

The need of such a barrier against the sea was recognized at an early time in the town's history. There is a touch of the humorous side of history in the spectacle of Spain, having chosen this bit of Florida soil for a town, building first a huge fort to defend it from the attack of invaders, and then a great wall to protect it from the inroads of the sea. The records tell us that the soldiers volunteered their labor and contributed part of their pay toward the construction of the first wall. They were probably wise enough in their day and generation to understand that if the town were swept away their lazy occupation of garrisoning it would tumble into the sea too. The first wall of which we have any note extended only to the center of the town; indeed, the seawall in English times, 1763, as shown by

THE PLAZA BASIN.

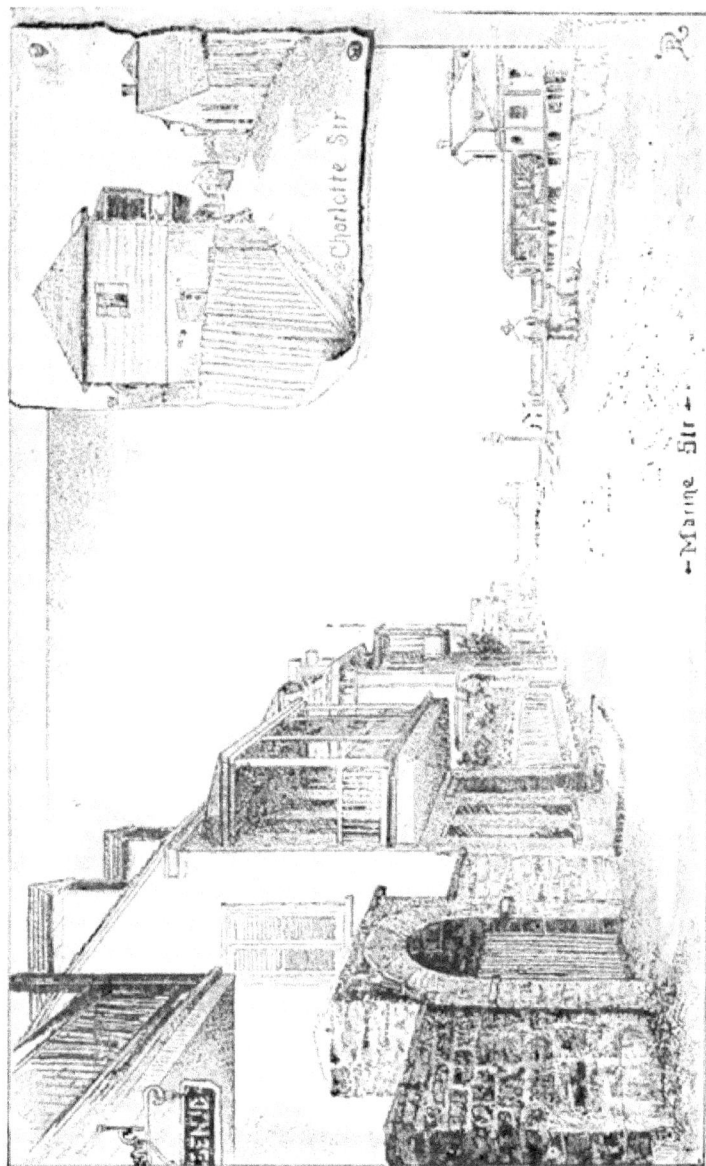

MARINE STREET AND SEAWALL.

a plan reproduced in "Old St. Augustine," was not carried south of the Parade (plaza).

The present wall was built by the United States, as a complement to the repairs of Fort Marion, 1835–42, at an expense of $100,000. Length, ¾ mile; height, 10 feet; width of granite coping, 3 feet.

At different points stairways descend to the boat landings at water level; and near the Plaza and Barracks are recesses or basins where boats unload their freight and find shelter from storms. These basins are gradually filling up, and it is not improbable that they will shortly be done away with, to the advantage of the street upon which they intrench.

From the seawall a charming prospect is afforded of the sail-dotted harbor, the shining sand dunes of the North Beach, the green stretch of Anastasia with the lighthouse rising against the eastern sky, and the quivering mirage of the horizon north and south. The wall itself harmonizes admirably with the Fort, of which it seems naturally to be a part, and its sweeping curves add not a little to the beauty of St. Augustine's water front.

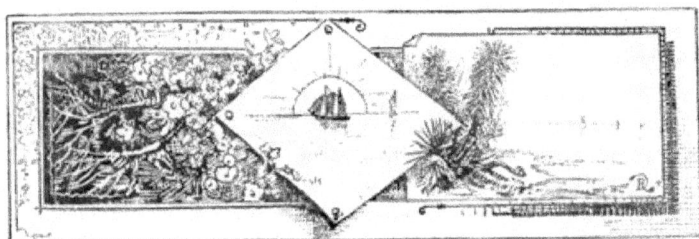

ST. FRANCIS BARRACKS.

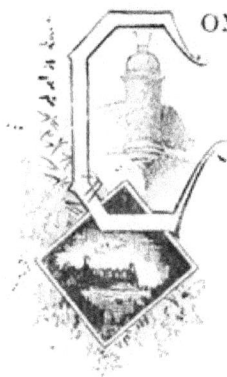

OMPLEMENTING the battlements and watch-towers of Fort Marion on the north, the St. Francis Barracks stand out conspicuously at the southern end of the town facing the Matanzas. Almost continuously since it was founded by the mailed soldiers of Menendez, St. Augustine has been a military post; and under Spanish rule it was little else. When the British came, they emulated the military spirit of their predecessors and built on the plain south of the town, with bricks brought from the banks of the Hudson River, a huge barrack, which cost a tremendous sum, and shortly after its completion went up in smoke. The present barracks occupy the site where once stood a Franciscan convent. This convent was abandoned when Florida was ceded to Great Britain in 1763; and when Spain resumed possession of the town, in 1783, the former convent was utilized by the Spanish Governor as a barrack for his troops. The old building has been greatly modified by the United States Government, although not entirely rebuilt; and some of the original coquina walls of the convent remain.

The post is occupied by United States troops. Two companies of the Second Artillery are stationed here, under command of Gen. R. B. Ayers. The out-door concerts giving by the military band,

ST. FRANCIS BARRACKS.

the dress-parades and the guard-mount at sunset, on the parade in front of the Barracks, are among the attractions of St. Augustine. Just beyond the Barracks, to the south, is

THE MILITARY CEMETERY.

For admission to the cemetery, the requisite pass may be had on application to the adjutant of the post, office opposite the Barracks. In the cemetery are the three low pyramids of masonry forming the tombs of officers and men who lost their lives in the Seminole War.

This memorial is commonly spoken of as " Dade's Monument," because more than one hundred of the soldiers interred here were those who perished in the " Dade Massacre." This was one of the most tragic incidents of the Seminole War. In the last week of August, 1835, two companies of United States troops, under command of Brevet-Major F. L. Dade, Fourth Inft., were on their way from Fort Brooke to Fort King, and while marching through an open pine barren were surprised and massacred by a band of Seminoles

⸺ in ambush under the scrub palmetto. This is the story as told ⸺ officer at the time:

⸺ rly on the morning of the 28th, the ill-fated party were again in motion, and ⸺ about four miles from their last camp, the advance guard passed a plat of ⸺ rass, and having reached a thick cluster of palmettos, about fifty yards ⸺ d the grass, a very heavy and destructive fire was opened upon them by an ⸺ en enemy, at a distance of fifty or sixty yards, which literally mowed them ⸺ n, and threw the main column into the greatest confusion. Soon recovering, ⸺ ever, and observing the enemy rise in front of them, they made a charge, and ⸺ their fire so unerringly that the Indians gave way, but not until muskets ⸺ clubbed, knives and bayonets used, and the combatants were clinched; they ⸺ finally driven off at a considerable distance. Major Dade having fallen ⸺ on the first fire, the command devolved upon Capt. Gardiner, and as he discovered the Indians gathering again about a half mile off, he directed a breastwork to be thrown up for their protection; but the enemy allowed them so little time that it was necessarily very low (only two and a half feet high) and imperfect. The Indians being reinforced, and having stationed about a hundred of their mounted warriors on the opposite side to cut off retreat, they slowly and cautiously advanced to a second attack, yelling and whooping in so terrific a manner as to drown the report of the firearms. The troops soon began to make their great gun speak, which at first kept the enemy at bay; but soon surrounding the little breastwork, they shot down every man who attempted to work the gun, so that it was rendered almost useless to them. One by one these brave and heroic men fell by each other's side in the gallant execution of their duty to their country. Being obliged, by the ineffective field-work, to lie down to load and fire, the poor fellows labored under great disadvantages, as in the haste with which the work was constructed they selected the lowest ground about that spot, and consequently gave the enemy doubly the advantage over them. Major Dade and his horse, Capt. Fraser and nearly every man of the advance-guard fell dead on the first volley, besides a number of the main column. * * * Toward the close of the battle, poor Gardiner received his death shot in the breast, and fell close to Lieut. Mudge. The command of the little post then fell on Lieut. Bassenger, who observed, on seeing Capt. Gardiner fall, ' I'm the only officer left, boys; we must do the best we can.' He continued at his post about an hour after Gardiner's death, when he received a shot in the thigh which brought him down. Shortly after this, their ammunition gave out, and the Indians broke into the enclosure, and since every man was either killed or so badly wounded as to be unable to make resistance, took off their firearms and whatever else would be of service to them and retreated." —" *The War in Florida,*" *by a late Staff-Officer.*

In the following spring 1836 a detachment of troops visited the scene of the massacre, and on the battle-ground where they had fallen buried officers and soldier. The grave was dug within the rude breastwork of logs; and at the head, as a memorial, they planted the cannon. Then the troops formed into two columns, and with arms reversed marched in opposite directions three times around the breastwork, while the band played the Dead March. But these military rites in the pine forest were not to be the final solemnities. At the close of the war, the remains of Dade's men and others were transferred to St. Augustine, and interred here, August 15, 1842.

The pyramids are stuccoed and perfectly devoid of any ornamentation. A monument bears, on the north, east, south and west faces respectively, the following inscriptions:

Sacred to the memory of the Officers and Soldiers killed in battle and died on service during the Florida War.

This monument has been erected in token of respectful and affectionate remembrance by their comrades of all grades, and is committed to the care and preservation of the garrison of St. Augustine.

A minute record of all the officers who perished and are here or elsewhere deposited, as also a portion of the soldiers, has been prepared, and placed in the office of the Adjutant of the Post, where it is hoped it will be carefully and perpetually preserved.

This conflict, in which so many gallant men perished in battle and by disease, commenced 25th December, 1835, terminated 14th August, 1842.

THE HARBOR.

AINT AUGUSTINE'S harbor, sheltered by the spit of land called the North Beach, and by Anastasia Island, is a sheet of water admirably adapted for pleasure sailing and rowing. These are among the staple winter amusements. At the wharves will be found a large fleet of sail boats, which are safe and commodious; and they are manned by capable and trustworthy skippers, some of whom learned to sail a boat almost before they learned to walk. Most of these craft are of local production, and built on a model peculiar to the harbor. Usual rates of hire, 50 cents to $1.00 per hour. In addition to these boats for charter, there are usually here in the winter sail and steam yachts from the North; and the private craft range all the way from the Minorcan fisherman's dugout (a survival of the ancient Florida Indian's rude log boat) and the clumsy wood-scows to the light and graceful Rushton canoe. A steamboat often seen in the harbor is the Seth Low, the famous tug which towed the Monitor down to meet the Merrimac at Hampton Roads.

An afternoon afloat is likely to prove one of the most pleasant memories of a visit to St. Augustine. What with the changing landscape—a shifting panorama of water and land and sky, the charming views of the town as seen from the bay, the bright sails in the harbor, and the multitudinous forms of marine life, there is always enough to interest and amuse. Fort Marion is well worth seeing from the water; the proportions of this fortification are hardly appreciated until one has approached the fort from the harbor its artillery once defended.

Extended excursions may be made see page 11' to Matanzas; up the North River; to Anastasia Island, Bird Island, and the beaches, called North and South with reference to the harbor entrance. North Beach is a term applied to the beaches of the ocean and the harbor and to the long narrow spit of land formed by them. Along the shores extend irregular lines of sand dunes, which are ever shifting and changing their shape, like the northern snowdrifts they so closely resemble. From the water or from the opposite shore the North Beach presents a scene of rare beauty, with its narrow strip of shining silver between the blue of the water and the deeper blue of the sky. Arrived at the shore, one finds half-buried wrecks and seawrack to dream over, sea shells to gather, innumerable forms of curious sea life to investigate, and the never ending, ever new study of wave motion and color. At sunset the Florida seashore takes on a peculiar beauty. Surf and beach are transplendent with the soft shades and delicate tints of the sky; the atmosphere is aglow with color, and there comes to one the novel experience of not alone beholding the distant glories of the west, but of actually standing in and being surrounded by the effulgence of the dying day. But the average St. Augustine skipper is not inclined to linger for sunset effects on the North Beach; the one practical consideration with him is that when the sun goes down the sea breeze will go down too, and his boat and party will be becalmed. Experience has taught him the wisdom of an early return to the wharves. Menendez, the Spanish founder of St. Augustine, had an unpleasant bit of adventure, brought about by this sunset calm. He had gone out in a small boat to one of his large ships, the San Palayo, lying off the coast, and on his way back to the new town at sunset he was becalmed and compelled to anchor outside the bar. When he woke up the next morning the first thing he saw was the French fleet bearing

down upon him, and it was only by hairbreadth escape that he
eluded his pursuers and in his little boat crossed the bar where their
ships could not follow.*

The porpoises which frequent the harbor in great numbers have
always been a conspicuous feature of these waters. Away back in
1563, before the Spaniards had founded St. Augustine, the French
explorers who came here found the porpoises or dolphins' so
numerous that they gave to the river the name " Rivière des
Dauphines," the River of Dolphins, and by this name it is set down
on the old maps. Among the Florida pictures by the French artist,
Jacques Le Moyne, who came here with that expedition, is one
intended to represent the French ships at the River of Dolphins;
this drawing is one of the five De Bry plates reproduced in " Old
St. Augustine," from which we borrow the copy on the opposite
page.

One charming feature of St. Augustine's harbor—the feathered
life—has almost disappeared. A few years ago great numbers of
birds of plumage frequented marshes, bay, beach and sand bar; but
the monomaniacs who conceive that all feathered creatures were
made expressly as a target for bullet and shot, have pursued the
birds with such scandalous industry that practical extermination is
the result. Buzzards, carrion crows, ospreys and gulls remain, but
even these are harried by the harbor gunners possessed of an indecent
mania to kill something. An abundance of legitimate game may be
found within easy access from St. Augustine; and there should be a
law forbidding the destruction of any bird in the harbor and waters
adjacent.

---

* " OLD ST. AUGUSTINE," page 2.

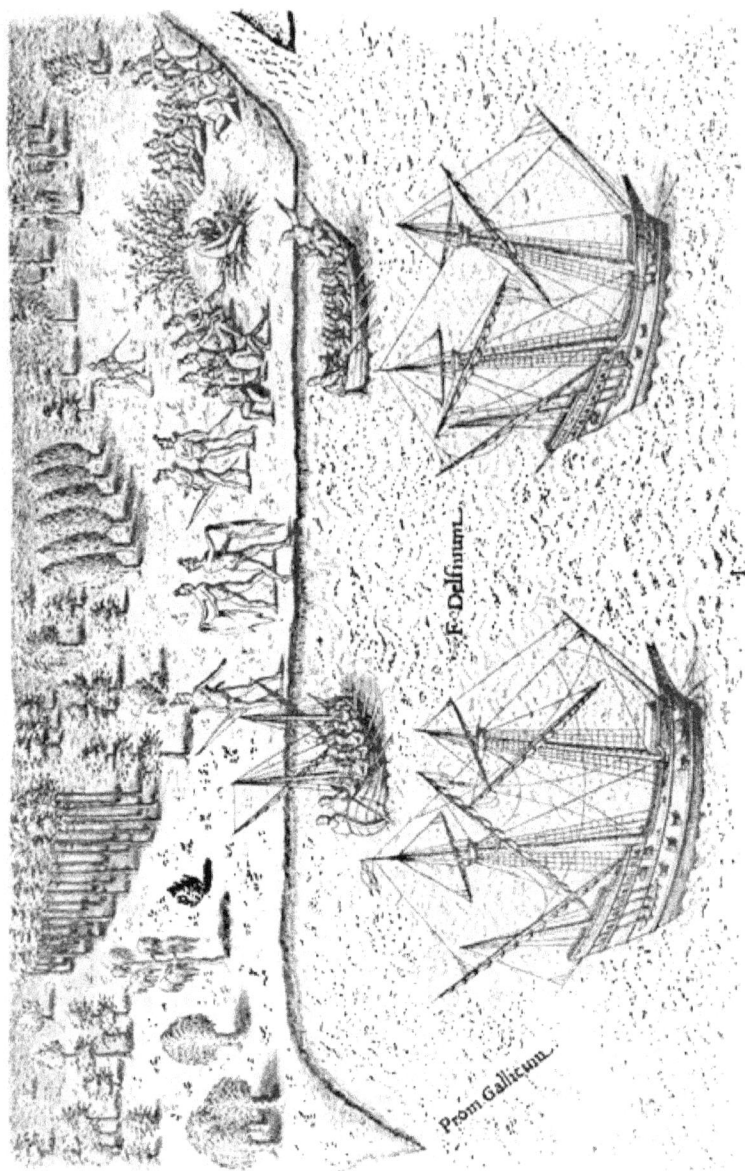

Prom Gallicum.

F. Delfinum.

RIVER OF DOLPHINS.

ST. ANASTASIA ISLAND.

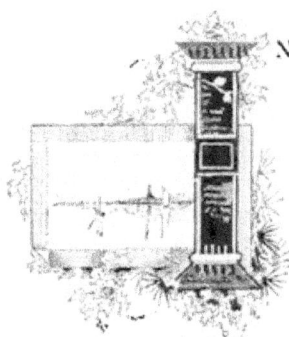

N FRONT of the town, between bay and ocean, lies the Island of St. Anastasia. It is a favorite resort for excursion parties, and has many attractions for the tourist. The most pleasant time for a visit is the afternoon. The route is by boat around the northern point of land to the beach direct; or, more commonly, across the bay to Quarry Creek (see map, p. 11), thence across to the light-house by tramway car, or by a charming footpath ¾ m. through the shrubbery from a second boat-landing further up the creek. Points to visit are the "new" light-house, ruins of "old" light-house, beach and coquina quarries.

The light-house is usually open to visitors; and when convenient to do so, the light keeper, Mr. W. A. Harn, or assistant, will accompany parties to the tower, whence a magnificent and far-extending view is afforded over sea and land. The light-house is 150 feet in height from base to light tower, the lamp being 165 feet above sea level. Eight flights of spiral staircases lead to the tower. The light, technically classed as of the first-order, is a revolving or flash light. The lamp itself is stationary, and the actual intensity of its

SHORE OF ST. ANASTASIA ISLAND.

flame does not change. The variability of the light is secured by
the revolving of the glass lantern, which is provided with a series of
powerful lenses or gigantic bull's-eyes, each one sending out a
great beam of light. The constant and steady beam from each
lense revolves with the lantern. From St. Augustine at night this
beam may distinctly be seen stretching out into the darkness, as it
wheels in mighty revolutions about the tower. The purpose of
the variability is that the light may be distinguished from other
lights on the coast; and that the light-house may also be distinguished when seen in the daytime, its exterior is painted black and
white in broad spiral bands, like a Brobdingnaggian barber's pole.

The present light-house was built in 1872-3, to take the place of
an older coquina structure, whose ruins may be seen on the shore a
short distance northwest. The latter has commonly, though incor-
rectly, been called the "old Spanish light-house." Its original
purpose and use were not for a light-house, but a lookout or watch-
tower, "where is always watch kept to see if any Ships are coming
from Sea, and as many Ships as many Flaggs are hung out that ye
Citty may know it." The history of the old time lookout on Anastasia is intimately connected with the history of St. Augustine.
It was one of a series of watch-towers and sentry-boxes established
by the Spaniards along the coast, whence the watchmen signaled to
the town the welcome coming of ships from Old Spain, or the
dreaded approach of a hostile fleet. A token of weal or woe, in
those days the signal flag on Anastasia Island was as eagerly
watched by the Spaniards on shore as ever in these times the light
is looked for by ships at sea. Away back in 1586, thirty years after
the town was established, the rude wooden scaffolding here attracted
the notice of the English sea-king, Francis Drake, sailing along this
coast on his way home from pillaging the cities of the Spanish
Main; and he tarried long enough to ransack St. Augustine, and
destroy by fire whatever he could not bear off. On numerous subsequent occasions the town was thrown into consternation by the
signal flag telling of an enemy's coming; and in 1742, when the

ST. AUGUSTINE LIGHT

Georgia forces were led against
St. Augustine by Oglethorpe,
they captured the lookout—
then built of coquina—and established their batteries on the
Island here, on the western
shore opposite the Fort, and
across on the North Beach.
Shortly after Florida came into possession of the United
States, the Government re-
modeled and practically rebuilt the old Spanish lookout, and converted it into a
light-house. Its situation was
then at some distance back
from the shore at the beginning of this century the distance of the lookout from the
beach had been ½ mile); but
with the gradual encroachment
of the waves the shore was
eaten away, the distance from
light to beach grew less and
less, until the impending fate
of the building was so clearly
foreseen that the new light-
house was built, and the old
one, no longer tenable, was
deserted. The sea at length
reached the coquina foundation ledge of the ancient tower,
and one June night in 1880, in
the height of a furious tempest,

Old Light House

RUINS OF OLD LIGHT-HOUSE.

the walls swayed, tottered and fell with a crash into the sea. Of the entire structure only a fragment of the rear wall of one of the out-buildings and a vine-clad bit of the loop-holed enclosure are left standing. The coquina blocks of the tower and the keeper's house lie in a mass of ruins where they fell; and the site, above which in times past the welcome beacon flamed for ships off the Florida coast, is now submerged by the incoming tide.

The sea shore of the Island is known as the South Beach. The North Beach is opposite; and to the right, seaward, are the great stretches of sand which form Bird Island. This is of recent forma-tion. Twenty years ago it was at low tide an insignificant tract of barren sand, much frequented by waterfowl, and at high tide almost covered by the sea. It is reached by sail boat from the town.

The coquina formation of Anastasia Island is well shown in the ledges at the ruins of the old light-house. The strata may be studied here, but are better seen at the quarries, southwest of the light-house ($1\frac{1}{2}$m). Coquina (Spanish, *coquina*, signifying a shell-fish) is a conglomeration of shells and shell fragments of great variety of form, color and size. Ages ago these were washed up in enormous quantities by the waves, just as other masses of similar material are now left on the beach, where one may walk for miles through the loose fragments which, under favorable conditions, would in time form coquina stone. When these shell deposits were cut off from the sea by intervening sand bars, like Bird Island, they were in course of time partially dissolved by rain water, and firmly cemented together in a compact mass of shell-stone.

The coquina stone is soft, and very easily quarried. It is cut out in blocks to suit the needs of the builder. It hardens upon expos-ure to the atmosphere; and was once extensively used as a building material. As already stated, the Fort, the Gateway, the Cathedral and a part of the Barracks are built of coquina. Quarry Creek took its name from these coquina quarries.

At the southern extremity of St. Anastasia Island is the inlet of Matanzas, often visited because of its historical associations, its ruined Spanish fort and its fishing grounds. A steam launch makes stated trips from St. Augustine, and sail boats may be chartered for the excursion. A hotel affords lodgings (with cooking privileges) and a restaurant is maintained in the season. The inlet and adjacent waters are favorite resorts for fishing parties.

Leaving the Barracks on the right, shortly beyond on the left bank of the river, a beautiful site is pointed out as Fish's Island, an estate which has been in the possession of one family for more than a hundred years. The original proprietor was Jesse Fish, who came here from Flatbush, N. Y., away back near the close of the first Spanish supremacy, lived here during the English occupation, and remained when the Spaniards returned again.

Five miles below St. Augustine, on the right bank, is Moultrie. In British times this was the site of Lieut.-Gov. John Moultrie's plantation, Buena Vista. John Moultrie was one of the planters who came here from South Carolina when Florida was ceded by Spain to Great Britain. At the time of the Revolutionary War he was a pronounced Loyalist. His brother, William Moultrie, of Charleston, was equally active as a Patriot, and was one of the prisoners brought to St. Augustine from that city in 1780, and a strange meeting it must have been this between Patriot brother and Loyalist brother. When Florida was ceded to Spain once more, John Moultrie abandoned his beautiful plantation, and left the province. Like other plantations, this was fortified. Later there was here a regular work of defense called Fort Moultrie. One of the famous treaties made by the United States with the Seminole Indians was signed here in 1823; and the Government's alleged violation of the agreement then made was one of the prime causes of dissatisfaction that led to the disastrous Seminole War.

The remains of the Spanish fort are seen on the right bank as the boat approaches Matanzas. Its ruins are the most picturesque in Florida. In the early morning and at sunset the fort and its surroundings present a scene of beauty well worth the journey to behold. The fort is of coquina, and was built to defend St. Augustine from the approach of an enemy by way of Matanzas Inlet. It was among the Spanish fortifications enumerated by Oglethorpe when he wrote to the King of England for instructions to proceed against and destroy St. Augustine. During the second Spanish supremacy, Matanzas fort was occupied by a garrison of negro troops.

At Matanzas Spanish, *Matanza*, "place of slaughter" occurred the massacre of the shipwrecked French Huguenots by the Spanish bigot Menendez in 1565—an incident whose heartless atrocity has not been surpassed in all the three centuries of St. Augustine's remarkable history. It is probable that the shores of the inlet have been greatly modified since then, and it is, therefore, quite useless to speculate upon the exact locality where the tragedy took place.

RUINS OF FORT AT MATANZAS.

FLORAL CALENDAR.

ECAUSE of the pretty fable that the name Florida was given to a "Land of Flowers," and because the tropical features of the northern portion of the State have been grossly exaggerated, most persons who come here are quite apt to be disappointed when they find the floral display less profuse and brilliant than they anticipated. They forget that like the North, the South also has its seasons, which are marked in the same manner if in less degree. Spring is the time of bursting bud and blossoms; summer of luxuriant and maturing vegetation; autumn of the falling leaf; while in winter the Florida verdure is sere and brown, the deciduous trees are bare of leaves, and beneath the sombre drapings of tillandsia—as in the North beneath the sheet of snow—the earth rests and recuperates.

There is yet an abundance of foliage and color. Lemon, orange and lime, oleander, olive and magnolia, date palm, palmetto and bay are evergreen; rose gardens are in perennial bloom; and if one have an eye for wild flowers, their number and variety will be found surprisingly rich and varied, even in the winter months. Of the three hundred and seventy-five species to be collected within a radius of twenty-five miles, more than one hundred may be gathered in the winter season.

DATE PALM.

The climate is hardly tropical enough for successful culture of the banana, and as the growth of the plant is uncertain, no definite time can be given for its blooming; the blossom appears whenever the plant is sufficiently matured, whether this be in March or April, or at any time between. Many varieties of roses are grown in St. Augustine, the choicer kinds as well as more common varieties being constant bloomers.

Among the different roses, as noted in one rose garden on Cedar street, are the following : Constant bloomers and most hardy— Pink daily, Glorie de Rosamond, climbing daily and blush roses.

Constant bloomers except in frosty weather —America, Arch Duke Charles, Aline Sisley, Baron Alexander de Vrints, Agrippina, Comtesse Riza du Parc, Cloth of Gold, Duchesse de Brabant, Bougere, Isabella Sprunt, La Princess Vera, James Sprunt, Lamarque, Lucullus, Mad. Lawrence, Mad. Camille, Malmaison, Rubens, Marechal Neil, Perle de Lyon, Reine Marie Henriette, Sofrano, Beau Carmine, Solfaterre, Cels Multiflora, Doctor Berthet, Laurette, Louis Richard, Estella Prodel, La Grandeur, La Sylphide, Cornelia Cook, La France, Queen of Lombardy, Catherine Mermet, Perle des Jardins, Mad. Cecile Bruner, Triumph d'Angers, Mad. Joseph Schwartz, Letty Coles, Amazone, Duchess of Orleans, Queen of France. Among

BLOSSOM OF THE BANANA.

other garden flowers the bignonia and opoponax are in constant bloom.

The following list, which is not intended to be complete, gives the flowering of only some of the more conspicuous of Florida flowers:

WILD FLOWERS.

JANUARY.—Blue and white Violets, creeping Houstonia, late Asters and early Yellow Jessamine.

FEBRUARY.—In wet pine barrens: Utricularia, Violets, daisy-like Chaptalia and Pinguicula. In low woods: Yellow Jessamine, Florida Hawthorn, (Cratægus glandulosa) and Wild Plum.

MARCH.—In wet pine barrens: Huge Thistles (used for making pompons) Pinguiculas, Andromedas, Violets and Sundews; and the two orchids, Calopogon and Pogonia. Beside streams: Azalea, Dogwood and Viburnum. In dry barrens: Lupines, Baptisia, Andromedas, Huckleberries, late Yellow Jessamine and Ascyrum ("St. Peter's-Wort ").

APRIL.—In wet barrens: Sarracenia (" Pitcher plant "), Sundew, Iris and Pogonia. In dry barrens: Milkweeds, Polygalas, Vaccinium, Arboreum ("Sparkle berry"), "Coral Plant " or " Cherokee Bean " (Erythrina), and " Horse Nettle."

MAY.—Spanish Bayonet (Yucca), Magnolia, " Loblolly " or Sweet Bay Magnolia, Wild Calla, Rhexia (" Deer Grass "), and Tillandsia, or " Spanish Moss," (which is not a moss but an air-plant).

SUMMER.—Three kinds of Palmetto, Prickly Ash, Prickly Pear, " Spider Lilies," " Matrimony," Wild Rose, Wild Canna, Coreopsis, Lobelias, Passion Flower, six Polygalas, Lily, " Beach Grass " or " Sea Oats," etc.; among the orchids three Gymnadenias, four Platantheras, and an Epidendrum.

AUTUMN.—Four or five Liatris, several Golden Rods, Baccharis, Asters, Sabbatias, Eupatorium.

DECEMBER.—Asters, Baccharis, scarlet berries of the Ilex cassine, ("Cassine," " Christmas-berry "), Ilex opaca or Holly, and red and black berries of the Wild Smilax.

IN CULTIVATED GROUNDS.

FEBRUARY.—" Cherry-Laurel," wrongly called " Wild Olive," Orange Opoponax and Cherokee Rose.

MARCH.—Vetch, Mexican Poppy or Argemone, Amaryllis Atamasco, Linaria, Sorrel, Cherokee Rose, Opoponax and Yellow Pyrropappus.

APRIL.—Oleander, Pomegranate, Woodbine, Honeysuckle, Sweet Olive, Cherokee Rose.

SUMMER.—Century plant and Date trees, Crêpe Myrtle and Pride of India, Yellow Elder and Parkinsonia, wrongly called " Mexican Chapparal."

The Japan plum (Eryobotria japonica) blossoms from October to December.

M. C. R.

HISTORICAL.

St. Augustine founded by Menendez, 1565. Sacked by Drake, 1580, and by the Boucaniers, 1665. Besieged by Moore of Carolina, 1702. and by Oglethorpe of Georgia, 1740. Becomes a British possession, 1763. Retroceded to Spain, 1783. Acquired by the United States, 1821. Seminole war, 1835-42.

NTIQUITY is among the least of St. Augustine's claims to historical distinction. Its three centuries have been crowded with stirring incident and eventful change, and were this the place for it the story would be worth the telling. The town was founded at a time when every endeavor and achievement of Europeans on this continent savored of romance ; and among all the events of the period the establishment of St. Augustine by the Spaniards in Florida is memorable because of the incidents connected with it. No event in American history possesses more of tragedy and pathos than the martyrdom of the Huguenots—a band of men who had left their homes in France to establish in the new world a refuge from the religious persecutions of their native land, but found in Florida the intolerance from which they had fled, and perished at last by the hand of a bigot.

Massacre of the Huguenots. In the year 1563 a company of Huguenots sent out by the great French Admiral Coligny came to Florida and established a fort on what is now the St. Johns. Two years later they were joined by a second company, under command of Jean Ribault. These Frenchmen were regarded by the Spaniards as trespassers on Spanish territory—for Spain professed to have title to all of North America—and a Spanish fleet was dispatched to Florida to drive them out. The French under Ribault and the Spaniards under Pedro Menendez reached Florida at almost the same time. Menendez, after an unsuccessful encounter with Ribault's fleet off the mouth of the St. Johns, proceeded south, entered the harbor which had been named by the French the River of Dolphins, disembarked his forces, took possession of the country in the name of the King of Spain, and on the site of the Indian village of Seloy established a new town—the first permanent settlement of Europeans on the continent. After the Spanish custom of the time they gave it a saintly name, calling it after St. Augustine (Spanish, San Augustin , upon whose day they had first sighted the Florida coast.

Here then were the Spaniards; and forty miles north were the Frenchmen. The whole vast continent was before them ; but there was not room for both. One must perish.

The French, leaving a few of their number to garrison Fort Caroline, set sail against the Spaniards, arrived off the bar of St. Augustine, and were driven to the south by a storm. Menendez then led a force overland to the St. Johns, surprised Fort Caroline and killed most of the garrison—a few of the French escaping to their ships. Upon his return to St. Augustine the Spaniard learned that the French fleet had been wrecked. He proceeded south to an inlet—now called Matanzas—and discovered the shipwrecked Frenchmen on the other side. By false promises he induced them to surrender, and deliver up their arms. Then he sent them boats, brought them over, small bands at a time, bound them, blindfolded them, led them behind the sand hills, and in the name of his religion put them to death.

That was in 1565. Three years afterwards a Frenchman, Dominique de Gourgues, arrived in Florida with a small band of French avengers and took the Spanish forts on the St. Johns. Most of the soldiers of the garrison perished in the fight. The rest were hung.

Drake. In 1586, on his way home from the Spanish Main, Francis Drake attacked St. Augustine, captured, plundered and brandchatized the town.

The Franciscans. St. Augustine became the head of an extensive system of mission labors by the Franciscans among the Florida Indians. Many missions were established and the number of converts must have been very large. The savages did not take kindly to the restraints imposed upon them, and in 1597, at the village of Tolomato, near St Augustine, a young chief, incensed because among other grievances he was allowed but one wife, rebelled against his religious teachers, incited his tribe to revolt, and with great cruelty massacred the priests, striking them down even at the altar.

The Boucaniers. In 1665 a company of those strange sea-rovers, the French Boucaniers from Hispaniola, came here under the leadership of Admiral Davis, fell upon the town, drove out the inhabitants, sacked and burned the dwellings, and went back spoils-laden.

The English. When the colony of Caroline was established the English grant extended so far south that it actually took in St. Augustine. The Spaniards, on the other hand, disputed England's right to any part of the continent whatever, and for the half century succeeding Spanish expeditions sailed against the English colonies, and British expeditions came against St Augustine. Governor Moore of Carolina led his forces against the town in 1702, but was repulsed and driven back. When Oglethorpe brought out his Georgia colony, the Spaniards resented the new encroachments upon their territory, and the two colonies were at constant war. In 1740 Oglethorpe captured the Spanish forts on the St. Johns, and then while his land forces besieged the town on the north his naval contingent landed on Anastasia Island and for forty days bombarded Fort San Marco. The townspeople took refuge in the fort, where they nearly starved before the siege was finally lifted. The Georgia general at length became discouraged and withdrew. In 1763 Florida was ceded to England. St. Augustine was an important British military station during the Revolutionary War, and several attempts were made by the American forces to capture it.

The Minorcans. In 1769, during the British occupation, a colony of Minorcans were brought from Minorca in the Mediterranean Sea to New Smyrna, on the Indian River, south of St. Augustine. Deceived by Turnbull, the proprietor of the plantation, and subjected to gross privation and cruelty, the Minorcans at length appealed to the authorities at St. Augustine, were promised protection, deserted New Smyrna in a body, came to St. Augustine, were defended against the claims of Turnbull, received an allotment of land in the town, built palmetto-thatched cottages, remained here after the English emigrated, and in the persons of their descendants constitute a portion of the present population.

Second Spanish Supremacy. In 1783 Florida was retroceded by England to Spain, and the Spaniards occupied St. Augustine until 1821, when Florida came into the possession of the United States.

Seminole War. Disputes over the boundaries of the Indian reservations, quarrels over fugitive slaves, which the Seminoles were accused of harboring, led in 1835 to the breaking out of the Seminole war—the most costly and disastrous of the minor wars of the United States. At the end of seven years, in 1842, the Indians were subdued, captured and transported to the reservation assigned them, where the remnant of their tribe yet remains in the Indian Territory.